Brief History of Our Lady of Good Success and Novena

*I am Mary of Good Success
The Queen of Victories*

*Dolorosa Press
www.dolorosapress.com*

Mother Mariana of Jesus Torres y Berriochaoa

A Predestined Soul

Modern man is accustomed to believe only in that which he sees, and is used to judge persons by what they own and not by what they are. For this reason it is difficult to understand the isolated life of the cloister, amidst sacrifices and prayers, and in which many times Divine Providence makes its greatest revelations.

Mother Mariana of Jesus Torres, one of the founders of the Royal Monastery of the Immaculate Conception of Quito, was a great mystic who embraced the state of evangelical perfection according to the teachings of Our Lord Jesus Christ, by taking it to the degree of heroism. God chose her to be the depositary of a series of revelations in regard to the century in which she lived and also to future centuries.

Born in Spain, in Province of Vizcaya, in the year of the Lord 1563, Mariana felt from an early age a religious vocation. Her life, from the age of thirteen years old, was a continual communication with the supernatural. So it was that, with the permission of King Phillip II, she left her country, accompanied by her aunt, Maria of Jesus Toboada, and other religious, bound for Quito, with the purpose of establishing the first monastery in the Americas in honor of the Immaculate Conception. This Order had been founded some decades before, in Spanish lands, by a Portuguese religious, Saint Beatriz de Silva.

At this time, Catholicism was prospering in the Royal Court of Quito at a secure and victorious pace. It was the achievement of the faith, implanted by the fervor of the missionaries and served by the boldness of the settlers and the Conquistadors, as well as by the goodness of the natives. Of this glorious past, they left as a legacy for the Ecuadorians of today, a faith and an admirable piety and numerous Marian shrines dedicated to the Most Holy Virgin, which recall her apparitions and her countless favors. In some of them there are very beautiful images, highly venerated by pilgrims from all over the country. For all these reasons Ecuador can rightly be considered the reliquary of America.

In answer to a request of the municipal council and of the most important Ecuadorian families, His Catholic Majesty, Phillip II, sent the group of religious foundresses, headed by Reverend Mother Maria of Jesus Taboada, the King's own cousin.

Convent of the Immaculate Conception in Quito

The Infernal Serpent

The powers of hell cannot stand the spread of devotion to the Immaculate Conception throughout the world. So they unleashed a terrible storm that threatened to shipwreck the ship in which the Spanish religious were travelling. In the midst of the storm, Mother Maria and her niece beheld a monstrous serpent which, by stirring up the waves, was attempting to destroy the fragile vessel. The child Mariana screamed and fainted, while her aunt was beseeching God to provide assistance at that difficult moment. When she finished her prayer, the storm miraculously ceased. Nevertheless, at sunrise, the sound of a terrifying voice was heard saying, "I will not allow the Foundation; I will not allow it to develop; I will not allow it to last until the end of time and I will persecute it at every moment!"

At their arrival in Quito on December 30, 1576, the Spanish foundresses were received with great jubilation and they lodged in the monastery whose cloister wall was still under construction. Very soon, motivated by a growing fervor, several young women of the city began to be admitted to the convent life.

Foundation

On January 13, 1577, the Royal Monastery of the Immaculate Conception of Quito was founded, the first convent of cloistered nuns in Ecuador and the first convent of the Conceptionists in Latin American, when a frail Franciscan received the religious profession of the six foundresses. They were the first spouses of Our Lord Jesus Christ in the Ecuadorian lands. The child Mariana Torres was not professed in the aforesaid ceremony simply because she was only thirteen years old. She would do this two years later, at the age of fifteen, receiving the name of Sister Mariana of Jesus. In this blessed cloister took place during the following fifty-nine years, the long Way of the Cross of this great religious, formed under the shadow of the Cross and transformed into an expiatory victim of Divine Justice.

Sister Mariana had to face the rebellion of some very bad nuns who, filled up with hatred by the devil, turned against her, calumniated her, and

Statue of Our Lady of Good Success in the choir loft, placed above the seat of the Abbess.

succeeded in incarcerating her in the prison of the monastery, in spite of her position as abbess. They considered her to be very severe and too demanding in the fulfillment of the Rule of Saint Francis which governed the Order of the Immaculate Conception since its origin. The rebels even came to the point of rejecting the Franciscans' direction, by plotting a conspiracy and obtaining from Rome that the monastery would be left under the direction of the local bishop. When the faithful religious saw the abandonment in which they had been left and the risk of extinction of the monastery, one day[1] Our Lady appeared…

I am Mary of Good Success

On February 2, 1610, at one in the morning, Mother Mariana was praying in the choir loft, with her forehead leaning on the floor, asking with insistent pleas the Queen of Heaven that she would alleviate the needs of the convent and of the young colony, and would come to the aid of the Church. In the middle of her fervent prayers, she noticed that someone was near her… a sweet voice was calling her by her name. It was a lady of extraordinary beauty, surrounded by a brilliance brighter than the sun, wearing a magnificent crown of dazzling brightness. In her left arm she was carried a Child, beautiful like the morning star, and in her right hand she was holding the keys of the cloister and a beautiful golden crosier, adorned with magnificent precious stones, as a sign of her ownership and authority over the convent. Being in ecstasy and overcome with emotion, the religious asked:

Who are you, beautiful lady, and what do you desire of me, who am merely a suffering nun?

With a sweet voice, the Lady answered her:

I am Mary of Good Success, the Queen of heaven and earth. Because you have invoked me with such tender affection, I come from heaven to console your afflicted heart. Your prayers, tears and penances are very pleasing to our heavenly Father… In my right arm I hold the crosier that you see, since I wish to govern this my monastery as Prioress and Mother… Satan wishes to destroy this work of God… but he cannot succeed, because I am the Queen of Victories and the Mother of Good Success, under which title I wish to do

Our Lady of Good Success gives Mother Mariana the measurement of her height for the making of the statue.

wonders in every age... I want you to strengthen your heart so that suffering may not defeat you. Your life will be long for the glory of God and of His mother, who is speaking with you. My Most holy Son teaches you suffering in all its diverse forms. And, to instill the courage that you need, I give Him to you. Take Him in your arms.

When she received the Child Jesus in her arms, Sister Mariana felt a greater desire to suffer and to consume herself as a victim to appease Divine Justice, if this were possible, until the end of the world. The most holy Virgin remained in the cloister until three o'clock in the morning.

Abbess of the Convent

Afterwards the Blessed Lady made known her will of being honored by the monastery as it perpetual abbess:

It is the will of my Most holy Son that you have a statue made just as you see me now and that you place it upon the throne of the abbess. And you will place in my right hand the crosier and the keys of the cloister, as a sign of my ownership and authority. In my left hand you will place my Divine Son. I myself shall govern this my convent.[2]

The most holy Virgin took charge of the convent as her own, assuring it a special protection against the onslaughts of the devil, further indicating that devotion to the Virgin of Good Success would obtain mercy and pardon for all sinners who have recourse to her with a contrite heart since she is the Mother of Mercy.

Measurement of the Statue

Mother Mariana hesitated. How can such a difficult task be accomplished? Firstly, how can the authorization be obtained from the bishop? Then, how can the resources be obtained, and what artist would be capable of sculpting the statue? "O Lady," insisted the religious, "how can all this be carried out if I do not even know your exact height?

Give me the Franciscan cord that you wear at the waist, the Virgin said to her.

At this moment, in the presence of the three Archangels, Saint Michael, Saint Gabriel, and Saint Raphael, who were showing themselves profoundly reverent before the Virgin, She herself took the cord and placed one of the extremities upon her forehead, telling Sister Mariana to touch her feet with the other end. But as the cord was very short, it stretched itself miraculously to the exact height of the Virgin.

You have now, my daughter, the measurement of your Mother from heaven; give it to my servant, Francisco del Castillo, describe my features and posture to him: he will outwardly make my statue since he has a delicate conscience and scrupulously observes the commandments of God and of the Church. No one else will be worthy of this favor. On your part, help him with your prayers and with your humble suffering.

Full of happiness, the religious took that precious relic and wore it during the remainder of her life.

The Virgin Insists

In the following apparitions, Our Lady of Good Success insisted again that Mother Mariana have the statue made as soon as possible, reprehending her for her delay. In order to convince her, she prophesized the future of Ecuador, of the bishop, and of other events (now fulfilled) such as the proclamation of the dogmas of Papal Infallibility and of the Immaculate Conception.

My beloved daughter, why are you so heavy of heart? ...How many hidden crimes are committed in this nation and in its neighboring regions? It was precisely for this purpose that this convent was founded in this place, so that God would be appeased in the same place in which He is offended and unknown; and for this reason the devil, the enemy of God and of the just, now as in the future centuries will make use of all his evil cunning to eliminate this convent.[3]

This very day, when the sun rises, you will go to look for the bishop and you will relate to him that I command that my statue be made to be put in front of my community, in order that I may take complete possession of that title, among many, that belongs to me. And, as a proof of the truthfulness of that which you will say to him, he will die within two years and two months, having from now on to prepare himself for the day of eternity since he will have a violent death.[4]

The Bishop

After much hesitation, Mother Mariana finally spoke with His Excellency Salvador de Ribera. The bishop immediately agreed:

Mother, why did Your Reverence not call me before? It is God Who so disposes and we ought not to ignore His voice and His calls. He is free to ask His creatures that which He sees fit.

The Sculptor

Francisco del Castillo, for his part, declared himself unworthy of being the sculptor of such a distinguished statue, indicating that he would do the work in the best possible manner. When he was asked about the price of this work, he answered that he would not charge anything and that he considered himself very well paid for having been chosen for such a sublime mission. He went to confession, received Holy Communion and on September 15, 1610, he began the eagerly awaited work.

He worked long days, always under the direction of Mother Mariana de Jesus Torres. The nuns of the convent were enraptured while watching him work. When there were just a few final touches left to do, he saw that the statue, although satisfactory, was far from representing that which Mother Mariana had seen. Francis then left on a journey in search of the best paints and varnishes to complete the work.

Upon his return with the paints, he was surprised to find that the statue had already been completed. Falling upon his knees, he exclaimed: "Reverend Mothers, what is it that I see? This exquisite statue is not the work of my hands! I cannot explain what my heart feels, but this can only be a work of the Angels, since a work of this nature cannot be accomplished on earth with a clay hand. Oh, no! No sculptor, no matter how able that he may be, will ever be able even to imitate so much perfection and such marvelous beauty." Immediately, in the presence of the bishop, he made a written oath testifying that what had taken place with the blessed statue was not his work, and that he had found it upon his return in a form very different from how he had left it six days before.

The Angels

What happened, then, during the time that the sculptor was on the journey? Who had performed such an extraordinary miracle? Mother Mariana describes the events as follows:

During the community prayers, on the afternoon of the fifteenth day [of January, 1611], God foretold to me that, on the dawn of the sixteenth day [of January], I would witness His mercies in favor of our convent and of the nation in general. He asked me to prepare myself for receiving these graces with penance and nocturnal prayers. So I did. The Archangels Saint Michael, Saint Gabriel and Saint Raphael presented themselves before the throne of the Queen of Heaven. Saint Michael bowing before her, said to her submissively: "Most Holy Mary, Daughter of God the Father." Saint Gabriel added: "Most Holy Mary, Mother of God the Son," and Saint Raphael concluded: "Most Holy Mary, Most Pure Spouse of the Holy Ghost." Immediately they summoned the heavenly legion and they all sang together: "Most Holy Mary, Sacred Temple of the Most Holy Trinity."

Heavenly Hands

Mother Mariana continues:

In this apparition Saint Francis of Assisi, accompanied by the three Archangels and followed by the heavenly legion, approached the half finished statue and, in an instant, remade it… giving it an incomparable beauty that human hands would never be able to give.

As Sister Mariana witnessed the paint applied by Francisco del Castillo slide down to the ground, the features of the statue became smoother and her countenance more heavenly. The Virgin was completely illuminated as though she were in the middle of the sun. From on high, the Most Holy Trinity was watching, pleased with what was taking place, and the Angels were singing their melodies. In the middle of all these joys, the Queen of Heaven personally, like rays of the sun entering into beautiful crystals, entered into the statue, which seemed to come to life, looked resplendent and with heavenly harmony, she herself sang the *Magnificat*. The Angels sang the hymn, *Salve Sancta Parens*.[5] All this happened at three in the morning.

In the morning of the same day, the sisters of the convent heard Angelic hymns and beheld the cloister completely illuminated with a heavenly light, and upon seeing the statue, they understood that other hands, another inspiration, had sculpted that marvel.

The Marchioness

It was still needed to provide the ornaments that the Most Holy Virgin had indicated would need to be put on the statue upon completion. So, the keys were made of silver. The Chapter took care of the crown of gold and the Machioness Maria de Solanda, a relative of the king of Spain, gave the crosier. When the marchioness was informed of the request to give the crosier, grateful, she addressed herself to the little Sister Mariana: "Mother, I would have been very resentful if Your Reverence would not have thought of me. Thank you for your attention and affection, and allow me to say that I will absolutely not permit anyone else to contribute to get the crosier of the statue of my Lady and Heavenly Mother. I will assist with the material and the labor. I can afford this and even if I could not, I would sell my property to get it. Please tell me how you wish that it be made and say no more! I will take care of the rest."

The Consecration

To comply fully with the requests of the Queen of heaven, Bishop Ribera consecrated the blessed statue on February 2, 1611, christening it with the name of "Mary of Good Success of the Purification or Candlemas." Preceding this event, the first novena in honor of such a glorious title was made and it finished with the solemn consecration. After anointing the statue with the holy oils, as is done with cathedrals or shrines, Bishop Ribera placed the crosier and the keys of the cloisters in the Virgin's right hand, handing over in this way the convent and all who dwell in it at all times to the maternal and loving care of Most Holy Mary. Thus was fulfilled that which Our Lady had shown to Sister Mariana: "Then, at that moment, I will take complete possession of this house of mine, and I will take care of keeping it from harm and free from all improprieties until the end of time, while requiring from my daughters a continual spirit of charity and sacrifice."

The Child Jesus of Pichincha

In the year 1628, Our Lady of Good Success said to Sister Mariana:
Raise your eyes and look towards Mount Pichincha, where my Divine Son Whom I carry in my arms will be crucified: I present Him with the Cross so that He may bestow good successes to this nation, which will be especially blessed, when I am known in all the land and they honor me under this title.

On Mount Pichincha, the Divine Child, approximately twelve years old and with a very beautiful face, white and ruddy, prostrated Himself upon the ground and said to His Father:

My Father and Eternal God, look kindly upon this small portion of the earth which Thou givest to Me today; grant that My loving and tender Heart and that of My Most Holy Mother may reign in it as two absolute owners.

Having said these words, the Child embraced the Cross, and crying, He was crucified upon it. His tears were collected by the Archangels, Saint Michael, Saint Gabriel and Saint Raphael, who scattered them throughout the nation.

The gaze of the young Jesus covered all Ecuador and while crying He said:

I could not do more for you to show My love.

Victim for our Times

The life of the Servant of God, Mother Mariana of Jesus Torres, was a constant series of Divine revelations, interventions and miracles. Our Lord God did not spare her anything that would help for her purification and perfection, since she was destined for her extraordinary vocation of being an expiatory victim for the sins of the world, particularly for those of

"I could not do more for you to show My love."
The battle of Pichincha was fought on May 24, 1822 in which six hundred men died, three hundred thirty were wounded from both sides combined, and one thousand, two hundred sixty Spanish soldiers were taken prisoner. Our Lady of Good Success had predicted that Ecuador would sever itself from Spain and become a Republic, and the Child Jesus appeared approximately two hundred years before where the decisive battle would occur.

Ecuador. The Divine Creator permitted that she would be tried very much by the devil, who frequently presented himself in the form of a serpent, prowling around her night and day. The fame of her sanctity had gone around all of Quito and its inhabitants flocked to her, calling her **little Mother**, in search of some supernatural favor. Her name had acquired enormous notoriety and the daughters of the time were baptized with her name. One of them was in fact little Saint Mariana of Jesus Paredes, born at the time of Mother Mariana, and who even participated in the funeral of the holy foundress at later date. In the middle of the mournful ceremony she proclaimed in a loud voice: **A saint has died!** During her life, Sister Mariana of Jesus Torres acquired the gifts of bilocation and of levitation; she cured the sick, reconciled families, and converted people. But without any doubt what were of greater importance in her life were the apparitions and revelations of Our Lady of Good Success.

The Revelations

The revelations that were made to her, above all, those concerning our days, are impressive for their precision and richness of details. Among the many details related by Sister Mariana to the bishop of Quito, there is something which tells us much regarding our days, namely, that her visions and her life would only be known beginning from the twentieth century, to help the souls of that time in which there would be **an enormous decadence of the faith.**

It is God's will to reserve this title and your life for that century, when the corruption of behavior will be universal and the precious light of the faith will be almost extinct.[6]

On December 8, 1634, the Queen of Heaven and Earth prophesied:

The consoling title of Good Success… will be the support and safeguard of the faith in the presence of the complete corruption of the twentieth century.

Prophecies Already Fulfilled

The Most Holy Virgin, in her messages, also sketched the map of the history of Ecuador at its inception and in the future. To substantiate the credibility of the prophecies, spanning different epochs, made by one person, it is a good rule to see if some have already been fulfilled and in what manner. In the case of Sister Mariana of Jesus Torres, the majority of the revelations which Our Lady made to her have had exact historical fulfillment.

Independence of Ecuador

During the apparition of January 16, 1599, Our Lady said to Sister Mariana:
The country in which you live will cease being a colony and will be a free republic, then it will be called Ecuador and it will need heroic souls to sustain it amidst so many public and private calamities.
This prophecy was fulfilled two hundred years later.

Consecration of Ecuador to the Sacred Heart

In the same apparition the Virgin affirmed:
In the nineteenth century there will be a truly Catholic president, a man of character, to whom Our Lord God will give the palm of martyrdom in the same plaza where this convent of mine is. He will consecrate the Republic to the Sacred Heart of my Most Holy Son and this consecration will sustain the Catholic religion in the subsequent years, which will be ill-fated for the Church.
On March 25, 1874, the heroic President Gabriel Garcia Moreno made Ecuador the first nation to be consecrated to the Heart of Jesus. In the following year, on August 6, 1875, he died, assassinated by the enemies of the faith, in the same Plaza of Independence on which the Monastery of the Immaculate Conception is located. His last words before expiring were: **God does not die!**

Proclamation of the Dogma of the Immaculate Conception and of the Assumption of Our Lady

In the apparition of February 2, 1634, Our Lady of Good Success placed the Child Jesus in the arms of Mother Mariana. The Child revealed to her:
The Dogma of the Immaculate Conception of My mother will be

Picture adopted by the Christian Statesman Garcia Moreno for the consecration of Ecuador to the Sacred Heart of Jesus in the year 1873. Moreno was assassinated in 1875. Father Mateo Crawley, founder of the Enthronement of the Sacred Heart in homes, adopted this image as the banner of his world-wide crusade for the social reign of that same Sacred Heart. He preached on that subject for fifty years.

proclaimed when the Church is attacked and My vicar finds himself a prisoner; and that of her death and Assumption in body and soul to heaven, when the Church has just gone out of a bloodbath.

On December 8, 1854, Pope Pius IX, amidst a terrible persecution against the Church, proclaimed the dogma of the Immaculate Conception; and on August 15, 1950, Pius XII, after World War II had ended, proclaimed the dogma of the Assumption.

Canonization of Mother Beatrice of Silva

In her spiritual testament, Sister Mariana of Jesus Torres, while speaking about the union of the Conceptionists with the Franciscans, says to her daughters:

Whoever pretends to prescind Francis [of Assisi] and Beatrice [the foundress of the Order] will not belong to the real and true Franciscan Conceptionist Order. And therefore, neither this holy Father Francis nor the holy Beatrice will recognize them as their daughters. She will be raised to the altars in the twentieth century.[7]

And so it happened: Saint Beatrice of Silva was canonized during the pontificate of Paul VI on October 3, 1976, that is, five hundred years after her death.

Prophecies That Are Being Fulfilled or That Are Yet to be Fulfilled

To indicate the driving force of the catastrophic crisis of the faith and morals which she describes in her prophecies about the nineteenth and twentieth centuries, Our Lady of Good Success mentions heresies in general and the sects, or simply the sect. These heresies or sects will have power to extend their claws to the home, by contaminating in a pernicious manner all the fields of human activity.

Corruption of the Children

...in what is now a colony and will then be the Republic of Ecuador, the passions will erupt and there will be a total corruption of customs,

for Satan will reign almost completely by means of the Masonic Sects. They will focus principally on children in order to sustain this widespread corruption... Woe to the children of these times! It will be difficult to receive the sacrament of Baptism and also the sacrament of Confirmation. They will receive the sacrament of Confession only if they remain in Catholic schools, for the devil will make a great effort to destroy these schools by making use of persons in authority...

...The sect, having taken control of all social classes, will be introduced so subtly into homes that children will be lost, while the devil will boast of being fed with the exquisite delicacy of children's souls...

...In that tragic time, there will scarcely be childhood innocence, for that reason priestly vocations will be lost and this will be a true calamity...[8]

Widespread Impurity

...the atmosphere will be saturated with the spirit of impurity which, like a filthy ocean, will inundate the streets, squares and public places with an astonishing liberty, in such a way that there will be almost no virgin souls in the world.[9]

Profanation of the Sacraments

I feel much pain in telling you that there will be many and enormous public sacrileges, and also hidden profanations of the Sacred Eucharist! ...My Most Holy Son will be thrown to the ground and trampled upon by dirty feet!

The sacrament of Holy Orders will be scoffed, subjugated and despised. Since by subjugating and denigrating God's Church, one consequently does the same to God Himself, Who is represented by His priests, consequently the devil will endeavor to persecute the Lord's ministers in every way and will labor with cruel and subtle craftiness to divert them from the spirit of their vocation... This apparent triumph of Satan will bring with it enormous sufferings upon the good prelates of the Church and the overall majority of good priests...

As for the Sacrament of Matrimony, which symbolizes the union of Christ with His Church, it will be attacked and deeply profaned in the fullest sense of the word. Masonry, which will then be in power, will enact iniquitous laws with the objective of doing away with this sacrament, making it easy for everyone to live in sin, encouraging the procreation of illegitimate children born without the blessing of the Church... During this time, due to the fact that in this poor country the Christian spirit will be lacking, the Sacrament of Extreme Unction will be little esteemed. Many people will die without receiving it either because of the negligence of their families or their false sentimentality towards their sick relatives...[10]

A Prelate will Restore the Catholic Priesthood

Priests will abandon their sacred duties and will depart from the path marked out for them by God. Then the Church will go through a dark night for lack of a Prelate and a Father to watch over it with love, gentleness, strength and prudence, and numbers of priests will lose the spirit of God, thus placing their souls in great danger. Pray constantly... that my Most Holy Son... have pity on His ministers and that He put an end to such fatal times, by sending to His Church the Prelate who will restore the spirit of His priests.

Upon this my beloved son, whom my Divine Son and I love with a love of predilection, we shall heap many gifts of humility of heart, of docility to varying inspirations, of strength to defend the rights of the Church and of a heart with which he will, like a new Christ, take possession of the mightiest of men as of the lowliest, without scorning the least fortunate amongst them. With a wholly divine gentleness he will lead consecrated souls to the service of God in religious houses without making the Lord's yoke weigh upon them. He will hold in his hand the scales of the sanctuary for everything to be done in orderly fashion for God to be glorified. This Prelate and Father will act as a counterweight to the lukewarmness of souls consecrated in the priesthood and in religion.[11]

"*Pray constantly...that my Most Holy Son...have pity on His ministers and that He put an end to such fatal times, by sending to His Church the Prelate who will restore the spirit of His priests.*" The late Archbishop Marcel Lefebvre directly referred to this prophecy during his sermon for the consecration of four bishops for the Society of St. Pius X on June 30, 1988.

The Root Cause and Final Remedy of the Crisis within the Church

Disastrous times will come unexpectedly, in which, by darkening their own clarity of vision, those who are bound in justice to defend the rights of the Church, without servile fear or human respect, will extend their hands to the enemies of the Church to do what the latter will want. But, alas, the erring of the wise man, the one who governs the Church, the shepherd of the flock which my Most Holy Son has confided to his care! But, when they appear triumphant and when authority abuses its own power committing injustices and oppressing the weak, its ruin is near. They will fall to the ground!

And happy and triumphant, like a tender little child, the Church will reemerge and sleep gently in the arms of the affectionate, capable love of my chosen son, much beloved in those times, to whom will be given the hearing of the inspirations of grace— one of which being the reading of the great mercies that my Most Holy Son and I have shown towards you— we will fill him with very special graces and gifts, we will make him great upon earth and even more in heaven, where we have reserved for him a very precious seat, because without fear of men he did combat for the truth and unperturbed he defended the rights of his Church, for which we could rightly call him a martyr.[12]

The Triumph of the Church

When all seems lost, there will be the beginning of the triumph of the holy Church.

After the impressive prediction of catastrophes for the Church and for Christian civilization, the Most Holy Virgin of Good Success promises at the end the complete victory.

… The small number of souls who will guard the treasure of the faith and the virtues will suffer a cruel and indescribable suffering, likened to a prolonged martyrdom…

…For the liberation from the slavery of these heresies, those to whom the merciful love of my Most Holy Son will destine for the restoration, will need great strength of will, constancy, courage, and much confidence in God. To put to the test the faith and confidence of the just, there will be moments in which all will seem lost and paralyzed. Then there will be the happy beginning of the complete restoration!...

There will be a great and horrifying war, in which will flow the blood of countrymen and of foreigners, of secular and regular priests, as well as that of religious. This night will be most horrible, since it will seem to men that evil has triumphed. At that moment, the time will have come when I, in an astonishing manner, will overthrow proud and accursed Satan, putting him under my heel and burying him in the infernal abyss, leaving the Church and the country free at last from the cruel tyrant.[13]

The Miracle of 1941

The statue of Our Lady of Good Success has protected the Convent of the Immaculate Conception of Quito throughout the centuries, and has been the pledge of continual graces for the protection of Ecuador and its inhabitants… **This devotion will be the lightning rod placed between Divine Justice and the prevaricating world, to prevent from being poured out the dreadful punishments that this guilty world deserves…**[14] So that her miraculous statue might be known throughout the country, the Most Holy Virgin produced the most extraordinary event that happened in Ecuador in the twentieth century.

In the year 1941 Peru had invaded Ecuadorian territory. In view of this emergency the Archbishop of Quito ordered that Triduums in honor of the various titles of the Most Holy Virgin be prayed in the different churches of Quito, imploring the cessation of hostilities. On July 25, the Triduum in honor of Our Lady of Good Success began in the Church of the Immaculate Conception. Three days later, from seven in the morning of Sunday, July 27, 1941, until three in the morning of July 28, that is to say, during twenty hours, the statue of Our Lady of Good Success moved its eyes. Its eyes were changing alternately from a reddish tone to another similar to marble. A type of mist was covering the statue. When this disappeared, it remained surrounded by a supernatural radiance. The statue's

The miraculous movement of the eyes of the statue of Our Lady of Good Success, signaling the ending of hostilities between Ecuador and Peru in 1941 made national headlines. The miracle was witnessed by more than 30,000 people.

eyes, which normally look downward, during the miracle raised themselves upward little by little until they remained looking towards heaven in an attitude of supplication; then they lowered towards the faithful, and repeatedly in this manner.

When the news spread, thousands of faithful invaded the church to gaze at the miracle, leaving the international events of enormous magnitude relegated to the second place. The maternal blinking of the sacred image was seen by more than thirty thousand people. On the afternoon of the same day, July 27, the newspapers announced the cessation of hostilities with Peru. The news relating the marvelous event came out starting the next day in the various newspapers throughout the country.

Últimas Noticias:	July 28, 1941
El Telégrafo:	July 28, 1941
El Universo:	July 28, 1941
El Debate:	July 27, 28, & 29, 1941
La Sociedad:	August 3, 1941
La Voz Obrera:	August 10, 1941
La Voz Católica de Loja:	October 5 & 12, 1941
El Comercio:	July 28 & 29, and August 3, 1941

Death and Glory

At three in the morning of February 2, 1634, Mother Mariana was praying in the choir loft when the lamp which burns next to the Blessed Sacrament went out. She tried to get up to light it, but an unknown force prevented her from moving. At that moment Our Lady of Good Success appeared, in the usual manner, carrying the Divine Child in her left arm and the crosier in her right hand.

Dear daughter of my heart... I come to give you the joyful news that within ten months and a few days, you will finally close your eyes to the material light of this world, to open them to the brightness of eternal light... Prepare your soul so that, purified still more, you may enter the fullness of the joy of the Lord.

And so it happened. The health of Mother Mariana began to decline, but she was still facing up to her duties in the convent as much as was possible for her. But the time arrived in which she had to stay in bed. Knowing the day and the hour of her death, Sister Mariana communicated to her beloved daughters the date of her passage to eternity: January 16, 1635, at three o'clock in the afternoon. She was then seventy-two years old. Around one o'clock in the afternoon of that blessed day, she asked the mother abbess to summon the community. When they arrived, Sister Mariana read in a loud voice her magnificent testament. With her voice trembling with emotion, but firm in the faith and with complete sincerity, she repeated the words of her beloved Lord:

It is expedient to you that I go but I will not leave you orphans. I go to my Father and to your Father, to my God and to your God, and the Divine Consoler will descend to comfort you.[15]

After receiving Extreme Unction, she tranquilly closed her eyes and ceased breathing. The Servant of God, Mariana of Jesus Torres, was now with God.

Four hundred years later, her body, as that of the other holy foundresses of the Royal Convent of the Immaculate Conception in Quito, remains incorrupt in the cloister of the convent waiting for the day on which, at the command of Our Lord Jesus Christ, they will rise unto eternal glory.

Her body is a visible testimony of the mission that the Most Holy Virgin revealed to her:

You have to be the sower of holiness in this volcanic land… your name will be known in all the continents of the world. And you will attain the honors of the altars… and you will be the most exalted protectress for this county consecrated to the Heart of my Most Holy Son.

A little more than three hundred and fifty years later, the statue of Our Lady of Good Success was canonically crowned with the permission of the Holy See on February 2, 1991.

Endnotes

[1] February 2, 1594.
[2] January 16, 1599.
[3] January 16, 1599.
[4] January 21, 1610.
[5] "Hail Holy Parent."
[6] December 8, 1634.
[7] January 16, 1635.
[8] January 20, 1610.
[9] February 2, 1634.
[10] January 20, 1610.
[11] February 2, 1634.
[12] February 2, 1634.
[13] February 2, 1634.
[14] January 20, 1610.
[15] Jn. 16, 7; Jn. 14, 18; & Jn. 20, 17.
[16] Cadena y Almeida, Mons. Dr. Luis E., *Memorial de la Coronacion Canonica a la Sacrads Imagen de Maria Santissima del Buen Suceso*, (Quito, Librería Espiritual), pp. 27-28.

NOVENA

TO OUR LADY OF GOOD SUCCESS

BY FR. JOSÉ M. URRATE, S.J.

Day One
Novena to Our Lady of Good Success

Act of Repentence
To be said first, each day of the novena

I believe in Thee, O my God. Strengthen, O Lord, my faith. I hope in Thee, O my God. Affirm, O Lord, my hope. I love Thee, O my God; increase, O Lord, my love. I repent of having offended Thee. O my God, help me to have contrition, so that with the help of Thy grace and the powerful patronage of Holy Mary of Good Success, I may never sin again. O Lord, have pity and mercy on me. Amen.

Opening Prayer
To be said each day of the novena

O most Excellent and Immaculate Queen of Heaven, Holy Mary of Good Success, most favored Daughter of the Eternal Father, most beloved Mother of the Divine Son, most cherished Spouse of the Holy Spirit, sublime Throne of the Divine Majesty, August Temple of the Holy Trinity, in whom the Three Divine Persons have placed the treasures of Their Power, Wisdom and Love!

Remember, Virgin Mary of Good Success, whom God hath made so great so that thou canst give succor to miserable sinners; remember that thou hast often promised to show thyself a merciful Mother to those who have recourse to thee. I come to thee then, Mother most merciful, and I beg thee, for thy love of the Most High,

that thou should obtain for me from God the Father a lively Faith that never loses sight of the eternal truths; from the Son, a firm Hope that always aspires to reach that glory that He won for me with His Blood; and from the Holy Ghost, a charity so inflamed that I will always live loving the Supreme Goodness and thee, Most Holy Virgin, until through thy intervention I will love and enjoy thee eternally in glory. Amen.

We salute thee Mary, as the Favored Daughter of God the Father.
Hail Mary...

We salute thee Mary, as the Chosen Mother of the Divine Son.
Hail Mary...

We salute thee Mary, as the Singular Spouse of the Holy Ghost.
Hail Mary... Glory be to the Father...

Day One

Consider how great and incomparable are the wonders of the omnipotent God Who manifests the treasures of His mercy for those He redeemed. Therefore, if we admire the excesses of His goodness in the many benefits with which He has enriched us, how much more should we marvel at and be filled with gratitude for the greatest blessing of His Right Hand, that most excellent and privileged creature, Mary Most Holy, whom He gave us for our consolation, especially to those who serve and love Him with all their hearts under the diverse titles and invocations that honor her. Through these devotions, we receive great favors by means of her succor and protection.

This has been the experience of true devotees of the Mother of God, and especially of those who have recourse to her by means of the marvelous Statue of Good Success, which was placed in the Church of the Royal Hospital in the City of Madrid. It was miraculous from its very beginning by virtue of the remarkable and unexpected way that this Treasure was found in the wilderness. As God said to the Prophet Isaiah, He would seek out those who had not come seeking Him, and would put aside those who had not considered His goodness or believed in His largesse. Thus also did the Most High make His Will clear that His Holy Mother is to be honored and venerated under the title of Good Success.

Prayer

O Lord of infinite goodness, by the miraculous making of this image of Mary Most Holy, Thou hast given us a powerful intercessor to whom we might have recourse with total confidence in her amiable protection in our necessity. Grant us the assistance that we are asking with fervor and confidence so that we might know, honor, and serve the Blessed Virgin, and so that by her intercession, we may achieve on this earth our sanctification and afterwards, be happy with her in Heaven. Amen.

Act of Thanksgiving to the Blessed Virgin
To be said each day of the novena

O Virgin blessed among all women! We lack the words to give thee thanks for the innumerable blessings that we have received from thy hand. The day of thy birth can be called the day of thanksgiving, happiness, and consolation. Thou art the honor of mankind, the joy of Paradise, the beloved gift of God, and the well-being of our country. What merit do we have, Blessed Virgin of Good Success, to deserve to have thee as our Mother? May God be forever blessed Who hath desired it so! Blessed also art thou, Virgin Mary, because despite our ingratitude, thou dost show us thy propitious favor.

Thus art thou, most clement Mother, our consolation on earth, our refuge, our help, and our protection in both our public and private needs. Safeguard us from war, pestilence, hunger, storms, earthquakes, and all the calamities that we merit by our guilt. Pray for the Holy Church and for her visible head. Hear the supplications of those who invoke thee. Be thou our Advocate, our Mother, for as thus do we place our confidence in thee. To thee do we have recourse, and through thy intercession we hope to achieve from thy Son pardon for our sins and perseverance in grace until death. Amen.

Here, each one raising up his heart to God, should ask, through the intercession of Blessed Mary of Good Success, that grace or favor which he desires to receive.

Praises to the Holy Virgin
To be said each day of the novena

O Virgin Mary, our Mother preeminent above all on earth.
Response: *Come to our assistance and show us mercy, because thou art our Mother.*

Above all others, thou wert attentive to the Word of the Father, Who doth great things in thy honor.
Come to our assistance and show us mercy, because thou art our Mother.

Thou art the most worthy temple of the Most Holy Trinity.
Come to our assistance and show us mercy, because thou art our Mother.

In thee is that same purity the Angels enjoy.
Come to our assistance and show us mercy, because thou art our Mother.

The Christian world proclaims that thou dost reign on the right side of the King of Kings.
Come to our assistance and show us mercy, because thou art our Mother.

O Mother of Grace, our Hope! Port of the shipwrecked and star of the sea,

Come to our assistance and show us mercy, because thou art our Mother.

Gate of Heaven, health of the sick, light in the darkness.
Come to our assistance and show us mercy, because thou art our Mother.

Through thee, we will find ourselves before God in the court of the Saints, where He lives and reigns forever.
Come to our assistance and show us mercy, because thou art our Mother.

Guide our steps and help us, O sweet Mary, in our last hours.
Come to our assistance and show us mercy, because thou art our Mother.

Receive this praise from our tender lips, which cannot express thy singular grandeur.
Come to our assistance and show us mercy, because thou art our Mother.

Antiphon: Holy Mary, save the miserable, help the weak, intercede for the afflicted, plead for the people, intercede for the clergy, petition for the faithful. Permit all those who celebrate thy holy memory to experience thy favor and assistance.

   V. Pray for us, O Virgin of Good Success!
   R. *That we may be made worthy of the promises of Christ.*

Final Prayer

We ask thee, our Lord and God, that Thou grant us health of soul and body through the intercession of the glorious Virgin Mary. Through her merits and those of her sovereign Child Jesus, we hope to be freed from the present evils and to attain eternal happiness. Amen.

Day Two
Novena to Our Lady of Good Success

Act of Repentence
To be said first, each day of the novena

I believe in Thee, O my God. Strengthen, O Lord, my faith. I hope in Thee, O my God. Affirm, O Lord, my hope. I love Thee, O my God; increase, O Lord, my love. I repent of having offended Thee. O my God, help me to have contrition, so that with the help of Thy grace and the powerful patronage of Holy Mary of Good Success, I may never sin again. O Lord, have pity and mercy on me. Amen.

Opening Prayer
To be said each day of the novena

O most Excellent and Immaculate Queen of Heaven, Holy Mary of Good Success, most favored Daughter of the Eternal Father, most beloved Mother of the Divine Son, most cherished Spouse of the Holy Spirit, sublime Throne of the Divine Majesty, August Temple of the Holy Trinity, in whom the Three Divine Persons have placed the treasures of Their Power, Wisdom and Love!

Remember, Virgin Mary of Good Success, whom God hath made so great so that thou canst give succor to miserable sinners; remember that thou hast often promised to show thyself a merciful Mother to those who have recourse to thee. I come to thee then,

Mother most merciful, and I beg thee, for thy love of the Most High, that thou should obtain for me from God the Father a lively Faith that never loses sight of the eternal truths; from the Son, a firm Hope that always aspires to reach that glory that He won for me with His Blood; and from the Holy Ghost, a charity so inflamed that I will always live loving the Supreme Goodness and thee, Most Holy Virgin, until through thy intervention I will love and enjoy thee eternally in glory. Amen.

We salute thee Mary, as the Favored Daughter of God the Father.
Hail Mary...

We salute thee Mary, as the Chosen Mother of the Divine Son.
Hail Mary...

We salute thee Mary, as the Singular Spouse of the Holy Ghost.
Hail Mary... Glory be to the Father...

Day Two

Consider how the providence of the Most High desired to so favor mankind by manifesting the hidden treasure of the precious statue of Holy Mary under the title of Good Success. After the death of Brother Bernandine de Obregón, founder of the Brotherhood of the Friars Minors for the Service of the Sick (the Order of St. Francis of Paola), Gabriel de Fontaned was elected to replace him. Accompanied by Guillermo Rigosa, he traveled to Rome to ask the Supreme Pontiff for his official approval of the Institute and the habit with the purple cross that distinguishes the order.

As they were passing through the town of Traigueras (under the jurisdiction of Tortosa in the Principate of Cataluna), they were caught in a terrifying hailstorm with lightening and thunder so strong that their hearts were filled with terror. They begged God to provide them with a shelter where they could take refuge so that they might prepare to die in peace, for the unrelenting rigor of the storm had persuaded them that they would not survive it.

However, God in His Divine Mercy so disposed that this search for shelter should be a presage of a good fortune. In a burst of lightning, they were able to discern a turnoff in the path. Following it, they could see the contours of a cave set in the hill above them. Even from the distance, they could see a bright light illuminating its interior and smell a sweet and heavenly aroma, more intense than anything on earth. Their souls were inundated with a great happiness as well as a sentiment of reverent admiration. At the same time, they felt an interior impulse to know the cause of such wonders.

Prayer

O God, admirable in all Thy works! May Thou always convert the most hazardous occurrences of life into proofs of Thy mercies, and in the most desperate storms may Thou show us the preludes to Thy prodigies in our favor, just as Thou didst with the Minorite brothers by means of that terrifying storm. Grant to us, through the intercession of the Queen of Good Success, the virtue of patience, to suffer with a resigned spirit the trials sent us by Thy Divine Will, because at any moment Thou canst change them to consolations in this life and afterwards grant us Thy eternal reward in Heaven, where we will always sing Thy praise and the praise of Holy Mary. Amen.

Act of Thanksgiving to the Blessed Virgin
To be said each day of the novena

O Virgin blessed among all women! We lack the words to give thee thanks for the innumerable blessings that we have received from thy hand. The day of thy birth can be called the day of thanksgiving, happiness, and consolation. Thou art the honor of mankind, the joy of Paradise, the beloved gift of God, and the well-being of our country. What merit do we have, Blessed Virgin of Good Success, to deserve to have thee as our Mother? May God be forever blessed Who hath desired it so! Blessed also art thou, Virgin Mary, because despite our ingratitude, thou showest us thy propitious favor.

Thus art thou, most clement Mother, our consolation on earth, our refuge, our help, and our protection in both our public and private needs. Safeguard us from war, pestilence, hunger, storms, earthquakes, and all the calamities that we merit by our guilt. Pray for the Holy Church and for her visible head. Hear the supplications of those who invoke thee. Be thou our Advocate, our Mother, for as thus do we place our confidence in thee. To thee do we have recourse, and through thy intercession we hope to achieve from thy Son pardon for our sins and perseverance in grace until death. Amen.

Here, each one raising up his heart to God, should ask, through the intercession of Blessed Mary of Good Success, that grace or favor which he desires to receive.

Praises to the Holy Virgin
To be said each day of the novena

O Virgin Mary, our Mother preeminent above all on earth.
Response: *Come to our assistance and show us mercy, because thou art our Mother.*

Above all others, thou wert attentive to the Word of the Father, Who doth great things in thy honor.
Come to our assistance and show us mercy, because thou art our Mother.

Thou art the most worthy temple of the Most Holy Trinity.
Come to our assistance and show us mercy, because thou art our Mother.

In thee is that same purity the Angels enjoy.
Come to our assistance and show us mercy, because thou art our Mother.

The Christian world proclaims that thou dost reign on the right side of the King of Kings.
Come to our assistance and show us mercy, because thou art our Mother.

O Mother of Grace, our Hope! Port of the shipwrecked and star of the sea,
Come to our assistance and show us mercy, because thou art our Mother.

Gate of Heaven, health of the sick, light in the darkness.
Come to our assistance and show us mercy, because thou art our Mother.

Through thee, we will find ourselves before God in the court of the Saints, where He lives and reigns forever.
Come to our assistance and show us mercy, because thou art our Mother.

Guide our steps and help us, O sweet Mary, in our last hours.
Come to our assistance and show us mercy, because thou art our Mother.

Receive this praise from our tender lips, which cannot express thy singular grandeur.
Come to our assistance and show us mercy, because thou art our Mother.

Antiphon: Holy Mary, save the miserable, help the weak, intercede for the afflicted, plead for the people, intercede for the clergy, petition for the faithful. Permit all those who celebrate thy holy memory to experience thy favor and assistance.

V. Pray for us, O Virgin of Good Success!
R. *That we may be made worthy of the promises of Christ.*

Final Prayer

We ask thee, our Lord and God, that Thou grant us health of soul and body through the intercession of the glorious Virgin Mary. Through her merits and those of her sovereign Child Jesus, we hope to be freed from the present evils and to attain eternal happiness. Amen.

Day Three
Novena to Our Lady of Good Success

Act of Repentence
To be said first, each day of the novena

I believe in Thee, O my God. Strengthen, O Lord, my faith. I hope in Thee, O my God. Affirm, O Lord, my hope. I love Thee, O my God; increase, O Lord, my love. I repent of having offended Thee. O my God, help me to have contrition, so that with the help of Thy grace and the powerful patronage of Holy Mary of Good Success, I may never sin again. O Lord, have pity and mercy on me. Amen.

Opening Prayer
To be said each day of the novena

O most Excellent and Immaculate Queen of Heaven, Holy Mary of Good Success, most favored Daughter of the Eternal Father, most beloved Mother of the Divine Son, most cherished Spouse of the Holy Spirit, sublime Throne of the Divine Majesty, August Temple of the Holy Trinity, in whom the Three Divine Persons have placed the treasures of Their Power, Wisdom and Love!

Remember, Virgin Mary of Good Success, whom God hath made so great so that thou canst give succor to miserable sinners; remember that thou hast often promised to show thyself a merciful Mother to those who have recourse to thee. I come to thee then, Mother most merciful, and I beg thee, for thy love of the Most High,

that thou should obtain for me from God the Father a lively Faith that never loses sight of the eternal truths; from the Son, a firm Hope that always aspires to reach that glory that He won for me with His Blood; and from the Holy Ghost, a charity so inflamed that I will always live loving the Supreme Goodness and thee, Most Holy Virgin, until through thy intervention I will love and enjoy thee eternally in glory. Amen.

We salute thee Mary, as the Favored Daughter of God the Father.
Hail Mary...

We salute thee Mary, as the Chosen Mother of the Divine Son.
Hail Mary...

We salute thee Mary, as the Singular Spouse of the Holy Ghost.
Hail Mary... Glory be to the Father...

Day Three

Consider how the travelers, impelled by grace and attracted by curiosity to examine such astounding wonders, set out for the site offering them refuge. Taking off their shoes, they climbed the hill with great difficulty, helping each other over large boulders and sharp cliffs. When they reached the cave, which they were able to see in the flashes of lightening, how great was their astonished joy and admiration! For they saw that this cave had been delicately carved by nature as a large temple. It protected a beautiful Statue of the Holy Virgin holding the Christ Child in her left arm and carrying a scepter in her right hand. A precious crown rested on her forehead. Her dress, like that of the Infant, was simple but elegant, and both were made in the same material and style.

The site, adorned with various types of flowers that carpeted the floor and climbed on the walls, filled the air with an exquisite fragrance for the Queen of Heaven. Set in the rock was a lamp so expertly crafted that it gave off the illumination of many lights. Such beauty and delight to honor such an admirable Lady! Such surprise and admiration for the overwhelmed travelers! The ecstatic pair contemplated this little piece of Heaven and calmed their overwrought hearts in the presence of their Mother, who after the terrible storm had come to them so unexpectedly, radiant with beauty and tender of countenance, to provide them with refuge and consolation at that desperate and difficult juncture.

So also my soul is calmed before the image of Mary. When the burdens of life and its imminent dangers bring us close to despair, let us go to her with tranquility and confidence, thanking God Who in His Omnipotence permitted this portentous statue to be miraculously found in that hidden place for the honor of the Immaculate Virgin so that all might venerate Her under that precious title of Good Success.

Prayer

O God of Mercy, Who never leaves desolate one who faithfully and fervently serves Thee amid the misfortunes and dangers of life, and Who leads us to find our Mother and advocate as a refuge in our adversities, grant us a tender and fervent heart to search for Mary and find her, always loving and protective, so that we might serve her and merit, through her intercession, to lead a good and Christian life and afterwards be with her forever in Heaven. Amen.

Act of Thanksgiving to the Blessed Virgin
To be said each day of the novena

O Virgin blessed among all women! We lack the words to give thee thanks for the innumerable blessings that we have received from thy hand. The day of thy birth can be called the day of thanksgiving, happiness, and consolation. Thou art the honor of mankind, the joy of Paradise, the beloved gift of God, and the well-being of our country. What merit do we have, Blessed Virgin of Good Success, to deserve to have thee as our Mother? May God be forever blessed Who hath desired it so! Blessed also art thou, Virgin Mary, because despite our ingratitude, thou dost show us thy propitious favor.

Thus art thou, most clement Mother, our consolation on earth, our refuge, our help, and our protection in both our public and private needs. Safeguard us from war, pestilence, hunger, storms, earthquakes, and all the calamities that we merit by our guilt. Pray for the Holy Church and for her visible head. Hear the supplications of those who invoke thee. Be thou our Advocate, our Mother, for as thus do we place our confidence in thee. To thee do we have recourse, and through thy intercession we hope to achieve from thy Son pardon for our sins and perseverance in grace until death. Amen.

Here, each one raising up his heart to God, should ask, through the intercession of Blessed Mary of Good Success, that grace or favor which he desires to receive.

Praises to the Holy Virgin
To be said each day of the novena

O Virgin Mary, our Mother preeminent above all on earth.
Response: *Come to our assistance and show us mercy, because thou art our Mother.*

Above all others, thou wert attentive to the Word of the Father, Who doth great things in thy honor.
Come to our assistance and show us mercy, because thou art our Mother.

Thou art the most worthy temple of the Most Holy Trinity.
Come to our assistance and show us mercy, because thou art our Mother.

In thee is that same purity the Angels enjoy.
Come to our assistance and show us mercy, because thou art our Mother.

The Christian world proclaims that thou dost reign on the right side of the King of Kings.
Come to our assistance and show us mercy, because thou art our Mother.

O Mother of Grace, our Hope! Port of the shipwrecked and star of the sea,
Come to our assistance and show us mercy, because thou art our Mother.

Gate of Heaven, health of the sick, light in the darkness.
Come to our assistance and show us mercy, because thou art our Mother.

Through thee, we will find ourselves before God in the court of the Saints, where He lives and reigns forever.
Come to our assistance and show us mercy, because thou art our Mother.

Guide our steps and help us, O sweet Mary, in our last hours.
Come to our assistance and show us mercy, because thou art our Mother.

Receive this praise from our tender lips, which cannot express thy singular grandeur.
Come to our assistance and show us mercy, because thou art our Mother.

Antiphon: Holy Mary, save the miserable, help the weak, intercede for the afflicted, plead for the people, intercede for the clergy, petition for the faithful. Permit all those who celebrate thy holy memory to experience thy favor and assistance.

V. Pray for us, O Virgin of Good Success!
R. *That we may be made worthy of the promises of Christ.*

Final Prayer

We ask thee, our Lord and God, that Thou grant us health of soul and body through the intercession of the glorious Virgin Mary. Through her merits and those of her sovereign Child Jesus, we hope to be freed from the present evils and to attain eternal happiness. Amen.

Day Four
Novena to Our Lady of Good Success

Act of Repentence
To be said first, each day of the novena

I believe in Thee, O my God. Strengthen, O Lord, my faith. I hope in Thee, O my God. Affirm, O Lord, my hope. I love Thee, O my God; increase, O Lord, my love. I repent of having offended Thee. O my God, help me to have contrition, so that with the help of Thy grace and the powerful patronage of Holy Mary of Good Success, I may never sin again. O Lord, have pity and mercy on me. Amen.

Opening Prayer
To be said each day of the novena

O most Excellent and Immaculate Queen of Heaven, Holy Mary of Good Success, most favored Daughter of the Eternal Father, most beloved Mother of the Divine Son, most cherished Spouse of the Holy Spirit, sublime Throne of the Divine Majesty, August Temple of the Holy Trinity, in whom the Three Divine Persons have placed the treasures of Their Power, Wisdom and Love!

Remember, Virgin Mary of Good Success, whom God hath made so great so that thou canst give succor to miserable sinners; remember that thou hast often promised to show thyself a merciful Mother to those who have recourse to thee. I come to thee then, Mother most merciful, and I beg thee, for thy love of the Most High,

that thou should obtain for me from God the Father a lively Faith that never loses sight of the eternal truths; from the Son, a firm Hope that always aspires to reach that glory that He won for me with His Blood; and from the Holy Ghost, a charity so inflamed that I will always live loving the Supreme Goodness and thee, Most Holy Virgin, until through thy intervention I will love and enjoy thee eternally in glory. Amen.

We salute thee Mary, as the Favored Daughter of God the Father.
Hail Mary...

We salute thee Mary, as the Chosen Mother of the Divine Son.
Hail Mary...

We salute thee Mary, as the Singular Spouse of the Holy Ghost.
Hail Mary... Glory be to the Father...

Day Four

Consider the indescribable joy of the good Minorite brothers on contemplating these prodigies. The Statue of our beloved Mother shone before them like a resplendent star, and they reverently prostrated themselves before her to praise and thank her for a gift so unique and an event so extraordinary. Their thoughts and sentiments were raised to heavenly considerations and they believed themselves to be favored by something supernatural. For everything they saw and felt within those walls of such inaccessible rock so far from any other houses seemed made by more than human hands. They repeated their prayers of thanksgiving with fervor.

Then, asking light and grace from Heaven to know what they should do, they decided to try to discover the origin of that sanctuary and Statue by seeking the pious persons or community who were caring so prodigiously for this cult. Even though it seemed impossible to them that such magnificence was the work of men in a place so retired and inaccessible, prudence and piety cautioned them to first make a careful investigation about the matter. They inquired at the hamlets nearest the cave, which were more than three leagues in distance, but found no one who could give them even the least information about the Statue. Not even the persons they questioned who were 80 and 100 years old had ever heard about the statue or any such devotion in those outlying woods or any other place near the region.

Consider, then, the astonishment and holy joy of the Brothers, now the owners of the extraordinary finding, as they humbled themselves again before the Holy Statue, offering her their warmest thanks with embraces and warm emotion, choosing her as their special patron and mediatrix under the very significant title of Mother of Good Success. The heart is moved by sentiments of pious gratitude and admiration for such a prodigious favor as this that was granted to the Holy Brothers.

Let us unite with them in their tender embraces of Mary, loving her and lavishing her with generous resolutions, because we also have mercifully found her on the dangerous pathway of life amidst the horror of the storm of our passions.

Prayer

O God of infinite love! Thou hast given us in our Mother a precious shelter and consolation, placing her in the pathway of our hazardous lives so that she might be a shield to defend us in persecutions and dangers as Our Mother of Good Success. Thankful for Thy goodness, may we correspond with the practice of virtue and a tender and constant devotion to Mary Most Holy, so that through her intercession we might find Heaven. Amen.

Act of Thanksgiving to the Blessed Virgin
To be said each day of the novena

O Virgin blessed among all women! We lack the words to give thee thanks for the innumerable blessings that we have received from thy hand. The day of thy birth can be called the day of thanksgiving, happiness, and consolation. Thou art the honor of mankind, the joy of Paradise, the beloved gift of God, and the well-being of our country. What merit do we have, Blessed Virgin of Good Success, to deserve to have thee as our Mother? May God be forever blessed Who hath desired it so! Blessed also art thou, Virgin Mary, because despite our ingratitude, thou dost show us thy propitious favor.

Thus art thou, most clement Mother, our consolation on earth, our refuge, our help, and our protection in both our public and private needs. Safeguard us from war, pestilence, hunger, storms, earthquakes, and all the calamities that we merit by our guilt. Pray for the Holy Church and for her visible head. Hear the supplications of those who invoke thee. Be thou our Advocate, our Mother, for as thus do we place our confidence in thee. To thee do we have recourse, and through thy intercession we hope to achieve from thy Son pardon for our sins and perseverance in grace until death. Amen.

Here, each one raising up his heart to God, should ask, through the intercession of Blessed Mary of Good Success, that grace or favor which he desires to receive.

Praises to the Holy Virgin
To be said each day of the novena

O Virgin Mary, our Mother pre-eminent above all on earth.
Response: *Come to our assistance and show us mercy, because thou art our Mother.*

Above all others, thou wert attentive to the Word of the Father, Who doth great things in thy honor.
Come to our assistance and show us mercy, because thou art our Mother.

Thou art the most worthy temple of the Most Holy Trinity.
Come to our assistance and show us mercy, because thou art our Mother.

In thee is that same purity the Angels enjoy.
Come to our assistance and show us mercy, because thou art our Mother.

The Christian world proclaims that thou dost reign on the right side of the King of Kings.
Come to our assistance and show us mercy, because thou art our Mother.

O Mother of Grace! O our hope! Port of the shipwrecked and star of the sea,
Come to our assistance and show us mercy, because thou art our Mother.

Gate of Heaven, health of the sick, light in the darkness.
Come to our assistance and show us mercy, because thou art our Mother.

Through thee, we will find ourselves before God in the court of the Saints, where He lives and reigns forever.
Come to our assistance and show us mercy, because thou art our Mother.

Guide our steps and help us, O sweet Mary, in our last hours.
Come to our assistance and show us mercy, because thou art our Mother.

Receive this praise from our tender lips, which cannot express thy singular grandeur.
Come to our assistance and show us mercy, because thou art our Mother.

Antiphon: Holy Mary, save the miserable, help the weak, intercede for the afflicted, plead for the people, intercede for the clergy, petition for the faithful. Permit all those who celebrate thy holy memory to experience thy favor and assistance.

V. Pray for us, O Virgin of Good Success!
R. *That we may be made worthy of the promises of Christ.*

Final Prayer

We ask thee, our Lord and God, that Thou grant us health of soul and body through the intercession of the glorious Virgin Mary. Through her merits and those of her sovereign Child Jesus, we hope to be freed from the present evils and to attain eternal happiness. Amen.

Day Five
Novena to Our Lady of Good Success

Act of Repentence
To be said first, each day of the novena

I believe in Thee, O my God. Strengthen, O Lord, my faith. I hope in Thee, O my God. Affirm, O Lord, my hope. I love Thee, O my God; increase, O Lord, my love. I repent of having offended Thee. O my God, help me to have contrition, so that with the help of Thy grace and the powerful patronage of Holy Mary of Good Success, I may never sin again. O Lord, have pity and mercy on me. Amen.

Opening Prayer
To be said each day of the novena

O most Excellent and Immaculate Queen of Heaven, Holy Mary of Good Success, most favored Daughter of the Eternal Father, most beloved Mother of the Divine Son, most cherished Spouse of the Holy Spirit, sublime Throne of the Divine Majesty, August Temple of the Holy Trinity, in whom the Three Divine Persons have placed the treasures of Their Power, Wisdom and Love!

Remember, Virgin Mary of Good Success, whom God hath made so great so that thou canst give succor to miserable sinners; remember that thou hast often promised to show thyself a merciful Mother to those who have recourse to thee. I come to thee then,

Mother most merciful, and I beg thee, for thy love of the Most High, that thou should obtain for me from God the Father a lively Faith that never loses sight of the eternal truths; from the Son, a firm Hope that always aspires to reach that glory that He won for me with His Blood; and from the Holy Ghost, a charity so inflamed that I will always live loving the Supreme Goodness and thee, Most Holy Virgin, until through thy intervention I will love and enjoy thee eternally in glory. Amen.

We salute thee Mary, as the Favored Daughter of God the Father.
Hail Mary...

We salute thee Mary, as the Chosen Mother of the Divine Son.
Hail Mary...

We salute thee Mary, as the Singular Spouse of the Holy Ghost.
Hail Mary... Glory be to the Father...

Day Five

Consider how the holy travelers, now convinced that their precious discovery belonged to them, placed the Statue in a basket, and with this so amiable and powerful companion they continued easily and happily on their trip to Rome, where they were received by His Holiness Paul V, a very chaste and pious man. They informed him of how they had found the Statue of the Virgin. Seeing her so precious and radiating with a supernatural presence, he prostrated himself before her, and hung his precious gold and enamel pectoral around her neck, granting graces and indulgences to all who venerated her.

He charged the fortunate religious who had found the image in such a marvelous way to honor the statue and zealously spread devotion to her in all corners. They saw in this, and even in the name of Our Lady of Good Success that the Pope gave her, all the signs that this was a supernatural discovery. This prodigious gift soon became an inexhaustible source of graces and wonders, which were experienced by the inhabitants of the city of Valencia where the religious brothers took her. Later the Statue was transferred with solemn splendor to the magnificent Church of Madrid, the capitol of Spain, where the venerated Statue continues to work wonders, her cult extending throughout Europe and even to the farthest regions of our America.

Animate yourself, my soul, in the presence of Mary, that this encounter might carry you through the most difficult junctures of life, with her sweet and smiling visage offering consolation. See, then, the Holy Father of the faithful prostrate in her presence, offering you this most priceless treasure and charging you to be devout and faithful in the service of Mary. Be content with the state in which God has placed you because you have Mary, who serves you as companion and protectress. Praise her, bless her, and present her with the pectoral of your love, placing at her feet your dominant passion, offering your efforts to overcome yourself with determination and constancy in order to obtain the exceptional favors that so many pious people have received from this Holy Statue of Good Success.

Prayer

O Sovereign God! Thou hast given us Thy highest counsel, the Most Holy Virgin of Good Success, as a companion to accompany us in our pilgrimage, so that she might serve us as guide, guard, and protectress in its conflicts. We go, then, to her, filled with confidence and finding the way easily on the journey to the dwelling of our Eternal Father, where all that we desire will be granted. Enflame our hearts with love for the Most Holy Virgin of Good Success so we might offer them to this Holy Mother with the gift of gratitude, a firm and constant love, and the conquering of our passions by means of the great graces received from Thy merciful Hands. Thus might we always have her favor in this life and her sweet assistance at death so that we might merit eternal salvation. Amen.

Act of Thanksgiving to the Blessed Virgin
To be said each day of the novena

O Virgin blessed among all women! We lack the words to give thee thanks for the innumerable blessings that we have received from thy hand. The day of thy birth can be called the day of thanksgiving, happiness, and consolation. Thou art the honor of mankind, the joy of Paradise, the beloved gift of God, and the well-being of our country. What merit do we have, Blessed Virgin of Good Success, to deserve to have thee as our Mother? May God be forever blessed Who hath desired it so! Blessed also art thou, Virgin Mary, because despite our ingratitude, thou showest us thy propitious favor.

Thus art thou, most clement Mother, our consolation on earth, our refuge, our help, and our protection in both our public and private needs. Safeguard us from war, pestilence, hunger, storms, earthquakes, and all the calamities that we merit by our guilt. Pray for the Holy Church and for her visible head. Hear the supplications of those who invoke thee. Be thou our Advocate, our Mother, for as thus do we place our confidence in thee. To thee do we have recourse, and through thy intercession we hope to achieve from thy Son pardon for our sins and perseverance in grace until death. Amen.

Here, each one raising up his heart to God, should ask, through the intercession of Blessed Mary of Good Success, that grace or favor which he desires to receive.

Praises to the Holy Virgin
To be said each day of the novena

O Virgin Mary, our Mother preeminent above all on earth.
Response: *Come to our assistance and show us mercy, because thou art our Mother.*

Above all others, thou wert attentive to the Word of the Father, Who does great things in thy honor.

Come to our assistance and show us mercy, because thou art our Mother.

Thou art the most worthy temple of the Most Holy Trinity.
Come to our assistance and show us mercy, because thou art our Mother.

In thee is that same purity the Angels enjoy.
Come to our assistance and show us mercy, because thou art our Mother.

The Christian world proclaims that thou dost reign on the right side of the King of Kings.
Come to our assistance and show us mercy, because thou art our Mother.

O Mother of Grace! O our hope! Port of the shipwrecked and star of the sea,
Come to our assistance and show us mercy, because thou art our Mother.

Gate of Heaven, health of the sick, light in the darkness.
Come to our assistance and show us mercy, because thou art our Mother.

Through thee, we will find ourselves before God in the court of the Saints, where He lives and reigns forever.
Come to our assistance and show us mercy, because thou art our Mother.

Guide our steps and help us, O sweet Mary, in our last hours.
Come to our assistance and show us mercy, because thou art our Mother.

Receive this praise from our tender lips, which cannot express thy singular grandeur.

Come to our assistance and show us mercy, because thou art our Mother.

Antiphon: Holy Mary, save the miserable, help the weak, intercede for the afflicted, plead for the people, intercede for the clergy, petition for the faithful. Permit all those who celebrate thy holy memory to experience thy favor and assistance.

V. Pray for us, O Virgin of Good Success!
R. *That we may be made worthy of the promises of Christ.*

Final Prayer

We ask thee, our Lord and God, that Thou grant us health of soul and body through the intercession of the glorious Virgin Mary. Through her merits and those of her sovereign Child Jesus, we hope to be freed from the present evils and to attain eternal happiness. Amen.

Day Six
Novena to Our Lady of Good Success

Act of Repentence
To be said first, each day of the novena

I believe in Thee, O my God. Strengthen, O Lord, my faith. I hope in Thee, O my God. Affirm, O Lord, my hope. I love Thee, O my God; increase, O Lord, my love. I repent of having offended Thee. O my God, help me to have contrition, so that with the help of Thy grace and the powerful patronage of Holy Mary of Good Success, I may never sin again. O Lord, have pity and mercy on me. Amen.

Opening Prayer
To be said each day of the novena

O most Excellent and Immaculate Queen of Heaven, Holy Mary of Good Success, most favored Daughter of the Eternal Father, most beloved Mother of the Divine Son, most cherished Spouse of the Holy Spirit, sublime Throne of the Divine Majesty, August Temple of the Holy Trinity, in whom the Three Divine Persons have placed the treasures of Their Power, Wisdom and Love!

Remember, Virgin Mary of Good Success, whom God hath made so great so that thou canst give succor to miserable sinners; remember that thou hast often promised to show thyself a merciful Mother to those who have recourse to thee. I come to thee then, Mother most merciful, and I beg thee, for thy love of the Most High,

that thou should obtain for me from God the Father a lively Faith that never loses sight of the eternal truths; from the Son, a firm Hope that always aspires to reach that glory that He won for me with His Blood; and from the Holy Ghost, a charity so inflamed that I will always live loving the Supreme Goodness and thee, Most Holy Virgin, until through thy intervention I will love and enjoy thee eternally in glory. Amen.

We salute thee Mary, as the Favored Daughter of God the Father.
Hail Mary...

We salute thee Mary, as the Chosen Mother of the Divine Son.
Hail Mary...

We salute thee Mary, as the Singular Spouse of the Holy Ghost.
Hail Mary...   Glory be to the Father...

Day Six

Consider how the city of Quito and its oldest Convent, the Convent of the Conceptionists, also experienced the special favor of the glorious Mother of Good Success, who appeared prodigiously to Mother Mariana de Jesus Torres, a Spaniard and one of the Founding Mothers of this Convent, in the year 1610, after the Convent had already been founded for 33 years. This fortunate and pious sister was praying alone with tender devotion, imploring the help of Mary under the title of Good Success for the needs of her own soul, for her sisters in the cloister, and for all mankind. In the fervor of her pleas, made with such profound faith and confidence, she raised her eager eyes to Heaven, calling on her Mother to come and save her and grant what she humbly asked with sincere interest for the good of her convent and for all the Catholic Church.

Suddenly a refulgent light flooded the church, and the good sister fell into ecstasy. Her mind was overcome by a sudden astonishment and her heart was moved by an inexplicable joy. Her faith grew and her devotion increased as the light diffused before her astonished and dazzled gaze. A singular joy entered her heart, and she redoubled her pleas in an ecstasy of unlimited confidence.

Thus is the soul invited to leave the mean Earth and look to Heaven with the eyes of a lively and penetrating faith. Heaven opens a path for it to the light of divine clarity and inundates it with the splendors of divinity. "The just live by faith." So indeed do the just make their Heaven here on the lowly Earth, attracting by their faith the light that does nothing to diminish the morning stars.

Let us also strengthen our faith in the revealed mysteries. Following the example of true religious souls, let us see with the eyes of the intelligence all the actions of our lives, leaving aside all thoughts of this lowly material life and focusing our understanding with efforts of faith on the ways of Divine Providence. It is principally by prayer that we leave this earth and think instead on matters of Heaven, where the Omnipotent God and Mary, His Daughter, Mother, and Spouse, dwell, awaiting our humble entreaties as pilgrims who, prostrate at their feet, implore the graces that we need.

Prayer

O, inaccessible Light of Supernatural Truth that illuminates our being with its Celestial Splendor and leads us to Thee, having for guide and protection Thy predilect creature Mary Most Holy, illuminate our minds with the light of a firm and living faith. It was such a faith that moved Our Mother of Good Success to appear before the eyes of that blessed Conceptionist religious Mother Mariana de Jesus Torres. Because we are anxious to enjoy supernatural goods, help us to be less concerned about the things of this earth. With the protection of Holy Mary and a constant and sure faith in the revealed mysteries, help us to live contemplating the brilliance of our final end and anticipating the joy of seeing Thee and Mary Most Holy for all eternity. Amen.

Act of Thanksgiving to the Blessed Virgin
To be said each day of the novena

O Virgin blessed among all women! We lack the words to give thee thanks for the innumerable blessings that we have received from thy hand. The day of thy birth can be called the day of thanksgiving, happiness, and consolation. Thou art the honor of mankind, the joy of Paradise, the beloved gift of God, and the well-being of our country. What merit do we have, Blessed Virgin of Good Success, to deserve to have thee as our Mother? May God be forever blessed Who hath desired it so! Blessed also art thou, Virgin Mary, because despite our ingratitude, thou showest us thy propitious favor.

Thus art thou, most clement Mother, our consolation on earth, our refuge, our help, and our protection in both our public and private needs. Safeguard us from war, pestilence, hunger, storms, earthquakes, and all the calamities that we merit by our guilt. Pray for the Holy Church and for her visible head. Hear the supplications of those who invoke thee. Be thou our Advocate, our Mother, for as thus do we place our confidence in thee. To thee do we have recourse, and through thy intercession we hope to achieve from thy Son pardon for our sins and perseverance in grace until death. Amen.

Here, each one raising up his heart to God, should ask, through the intercession of Blessed Mary of Good Success, that grace or favor which he desires to receive.

Praises to the Holy Virgin
To be said each day of the novena

O Virgin Mary, our Mother preeminent above all on earth.
Response: *Come to our assistance and show us mercy, because thou art our Mother.*

Above all others, thou wert attentive to the Word of the Father,

Who doth great things in thy honor.
Come to our assistance and show us mercy, because thou art our Mother.

Thou art the most worthy temple of the Most Holy Trinity.
Come to our assistance and show us mercy, because thou art our Mother.

In thee is that same purity the Angels enjoy.
Come to our assistance and show us mercy, because thou art our Mother.

The Christian world proclaims that thou dost reign on the right side of the King of Kings.
Come to our assistance and show us mercy, because thou art our Mother.

O Mother of Grace! O our hope! Port of the shipwrecked and star of the sea,
Come to our assistance and show us mercy, because thou art our Mother.

Gate of Heaven, health of the sick, light in the darkness.
Come to our assistance and show us mercy, because thou art our Mother.

Through thee, we will find ourselves before God in the court of the Saints, where He lives and reigns forever.
Come to our assistance and show us mercy, because thou art our Mother.

Guide our steps and help us, O sweet Mary, in our last hours.
Come to our assistance and show us mercy, because thou art our Mother.

Receive this praise from our tender lips, which cannot express thy singular grandeur.
Come to our assistance and show us mercy, because thou art our Mother.

Antiphon: Holy Mary, save the miserable, help the weak, intercede for the afflicted, plead for the people, intercede for the clergy, petition for the faithful. Permit all those who celebrate thy holy memory to experience thy favor and assistance.

V. Pray for us, O Virgin of Good Success!
R. That we may be made worthy of the promises of Christ.

Final Prayer

We ask thee, our Lord and God, that Thou grant us health of soul and body through the intercession of the glorious Virgin Mary. Through her merits and those of her sovereign Child Jesus, we hope to be freed from the present evils and to attain eternal happiness. Amen.

Day Seven
Novena to Our Lady of Good Success

Act of Repentence
To be said first, each day of the novena

I believe in Thee, O my God. Strengthen, O Lord, my faith. I hope in Thee, O my God. Affirm, O Lord, my hope. I love Thee, O my God; increase, O Lord, my love. I repent of having offended Thee. O my God, help me to have contrition, so that with the help of Thy grace and the powerful patronage of Holy Mary of Good Success, I may never sin again. O Lord, have pity and mercy on me. Amen.

Opening Prayer
To be said each day of the novena

O most Excellent and Immaculate Queen of Heaven, Holy Mary of Good Success, most favored Daughter of the Eternal Father, most beloved Mother of the Divine Son, most cherished Spouse of the Holy Spirit, sublime Throne of the Divine Majesty, August Temple of the Holy Trinity, in whom the Three Divine Persons have placed the treasures of Their Power, Wisdom and Love!

Remember, Virgin Mary of Good Success, whom God hath made so great so that thou canst give succor to miserable sinners; remember that thou hast often promised to show thyself a merciful Mother to those who have recourse to thee. I come to thee then, Mother most merciful, and I beg thee, for thy love of the Most High,

that thou should obtain for me from God the Father a lively Faith that never loses sight of the eternal truths; from the Son, a firm Hope that always aspires to reach that glory that He won for me with His Blood; and from the Holy Ghost, a charity so inflamed that I will always live loving the Supreme Goodness and thee, Most Holy Virgin, until through thy intervention I will love and enjoy thee eternally in glory. Amen.

We salute thee Mary, as the Favored Daughter of God the Father.
Hail Mary...

We salute thee Mary, as the Chosen Mother of the Divine Son.
Hail Mary...

We salute thee Mary, as the Singular Spouse of the Holy Ghost.
Hail Mary...   Glory be to the Father...

Day Seven

Consider how the fortunate religious, in the fervor of her pleas and illuminated by thet bright light that inundated her, fixed her eyes upon the source of that brilliance, finding before her a Lady of extraordinary beauty and kindness of face. As the light dissolved, she saw that the Lady was carrying in her left arm a Child, bright and shining like a morning star, full of grace and goodness, His features tender and kind. In her right hand she held a beautiful scepter of shining gold and precious stones, and around her forehead was a magnificent crown with dazzling stones. She wore a garment similar to that of the Statue (in Spain) of Mary of Good Success, whose miraculous discovery was recounted earlier and to whom the pious Conceptionist sister had been praying when she received the favor of this vision.

The good religious was at the same time transported with joy and confused to be thus visited by her Celestial Mother. Her soul was filled with a joy and gratitude without limit, and her heart flooded by holy sentiments. As thoughts of lively faith and valiant love and confidence overwhelmed her being, she asked, "Who art thou? And what dost thou desire?"

Then, o marvel of goodness! In a sweet and suave voice, the Lady responded: "I am Mary of Good Success whom you invoked with such tender affection. Your prayer has pleased me very much. Your faith has brought me here. Your love has invited me to visit you.

Ponder, o my soul, the singular privilege of this blessed sister, who merited by her faith, devotion, and fervor in prayer to attract the presence of Mary Most Holy and to thus contemplate her so lovely, so pure, and so beautiful, to be dazzled by her splendors, to enjoy her intimacies, and to hear her most amiable voice. Ah! Fortunate creature! How great was your love for your Celestial Mother! How strong your inclination to humble yourself and praise her! How ardent your desire to be with her! How continuous, attentive, and devout your prayers!

This goodness of Mary should thus encourage us to invoke her with deep faith under the title of Good Success and to pray always with attention and confidence, considering that only a living faith and vigilant attention in prayer will make us deserve to be heard and favored by the Holy Virgin, not with privileged visions, but with other gifts of grace that will help us triumph over our passions and the enemies of religion.

Prayer

O God of goodness, Who dost deign to reward the faith and zealous sentiments of piety of Thy chosen souls with visits of Mary Most Holy, hear also our prayers that the presence of this Statue of Good Success might illuminate our faith and increase our confidence that she will benignly hear our prayers. Grant us an ever increasing faith in Thy paternal goodness; make us ever more confident that we will receive what we ask for. Make us also ever more fervent in our prayers, so that supported by the great valor of our powerful Patroness, we might be freed from the dangers that threaten us, serve Thee better, and win the honor of being in Thy company and that of Mary Most Holy in Heaven for all eternity. Amen.

Act of Thanksgiving to the Blessed Virgin
To be said each day of the novena

O Virgin blessed among all women! We lack the words to give thee thanks for the innumerable blessings that we have received from thy hand. The day of thy birth can be called the day of thanksgiving, happiness, and consolation. Thou art the honor of mankind, the joy of Paradise, the beloved gift of God, and the well-being of our country. What merit do we have, Blessed Virgin of Good Success, to deserve to have thee as our Mother? May God be forever blessed Who hath desired it so! Blessed also art thou, Virgin Mary, because despite our ingratitude, thou showest us thy propitious favor.

Thus art thou, most clement Mother, our consolation on earth, our refuge, our help, and our protection in both our public and private needs. Safeguard us from war, pestilence, hunger, storms, earthquakes, and all the calamities that we merit by our guilt. Pray for the Holy Church and for her visible head. Hear the supplications of those who invoke thee. Be thou our Advocate, our Mother, for as thus do we place our confidence in thee. To thee do we have recourse, and through thy intercession we hope to achieve from thy Son pardon for our sins and perseverance in grace until death. Amen.

Here, each one raising up his heart to God, should ask, through the intercession of Blessed Mary of Good Success, that grace or favor which he desires to receive.

Praises to the Holy Virgin
To be said each day of the novena

O Virgin Mary, our Mother preeminent above all on earth.
Response: *Come to our assistance and show us mercy, because thou art our Mother.*

Above all others, thou wert attentive to the Word of the Father, Who doth great things in thy honor.
Come to our assistance and show us mercy, because thou art our Mother.

Thou art the most worthy temple of the Most Holy Trinity.
Come to our assistance and show us mercy, because thou art our Mother.

In thee is that same purity the Angels enjoy.
Come to our assistance and show us mercy, because thou art our Mother.

The Christian world proclaims that thou dost reign on the right side of the King of Kings.
Come to our assistance and show us mercy, because thou art our Mother.

O Mother of Grace! O our hope! Port of the shipwrecked and star of the sea,
Come to our assistance and show us mercy, because thou art our Mother.

Gate of Heaven, health of the sick, light in the darkness.
Come to our assistance and show us mercy, because thou art our Mother.

Through thee, we will find ourselves before God in the court of the Saints, where He lives and reigns forever.

Come to our assistance and show us mercy, because thou art our Mother.

Guide our steps and help us, O sweet Mary, in our last hours.
Come to our assistance and show us mercy, because thou art our Mother.

Receive this praise from our tender lips, which cannot express thy singular grandeur.
Come to our assistance and show us mercy, because thou art our Mother.
Antiphon: Holy Mary, save the miserable, help the weak, intercede for the afflicted, plead for the people, intercede for the clergy, petition for the faithful. Permit all those who celebrate thy holy memory to experience thy favor and assistance.

V. Pray for us, O Virgin of Good Success!
R. That we may be made worthy of the promises of Christ.

Final Prayer

We ask thee, our Lord and God, that Thou grant us health of soul and body through the intercession of the glorious Virgin Mary. Through her merits and those of her sovereign Child Jesus, we hope to be freed from the present evils and to attain eternal happiness. Amen.

Day Eight
Novena to Our Lady of Good Success

Act of Repentence
To be said first, each day of the novena

I believe in Thee, O my God. Strengthen, O Lord, my faith. I hope in Thee, O my God. Affirm, O Lord, my hope. I love Thee, O my God; increase, O Lord, my love. I repent of having offended Thee. O my God, help me to have contrition, so that with the help of Thy grace and the powerful patronage of Holy Mary of Good Success, I may never sin again. O Lord, have pity and mercy on me. Amen.

Opening Prayer
To be said each day of the novena

O most Excellent and Immaculate Queen of Heaven, Holy Mary of Good Success, most favored Daughter of the Eternal Father, most beloved Mother of the Divine Son, most cherished Spouse of the Holy Spirit, sublime Throne of the Divine Majesty, August Temple of the Holy Trinity, in whom the Three Divine Persons have placed the treasures of Their Power, Wisdom and Love!

Remember, Virgin Mary of Good Success, whom God hath made so great so that thou canst give succor to miserable sinners; remember that thou hast often promised to show thyself a merciful Mother to those who have recourse to thee. I come to thee then, Mother most merciful, and I beg thee, for thy love of the Most High,

that thou should obtain for me from God the Father a lively Faith that never loses sight of the eternal truths; from the Son, a firm Hope that always aspires to reach that glory that He won for me with His Blood; and from the Holy Ghost, a charity so inflamed that I will always live loving the Supreme Goodness and thee, Most Holy Virgin, until through thy intervention I will love and enjoy thee eternally in glory. Amen.

We salute thee Mary, as the Favored Daughter of God the Father.
Hail Mary...

We salute thee Mary, as the Chosen Mother of the Divine Son.
Hail Mary...

We salute thee Mary, as the Singular Spouse of the Holy Ghost.
Hail Mary...   Glory be to the Father...

Day Eight

Consider that the Holy Virgin, on appearing to the sister, did not desire to favor her alone with a single transitory grace, for God does not bestow His special gifts except with the providential plan of increasing the piety, stimulating the moral progress, and improving the religious discipline of all the members of a community, a country, or the whole Church. For this reason Mary Most Holy of Good Success told the Conceptionist sister, "It is the Will of God that I command you to have a statue made that will represent this apparition in all its details, so that it might be placed directly above the Abbess' chair in the choir where all the religious pray, so that they might consider this memorable Statue as their principal Abbess." Thus would this Statue stimulate perpetual gratitude, special attentiveness in prayer, perfect obedience, a firm faith, a confident hope, and an ardent love for Mary Most Holy who thus offered herself to preside over and govern this Convent.
Ah, if we had a living faith! With what veneration and respect would we place ourselves before that Statue! How keenly we would recall

her apparition so full of goodness and her promises and favors! How confident would we be in our supplications, how attentive in our prayers, how fervent in our devotions, how spontaneous in our obedience, how regular in our observance of the Commandments and the duties of our state of life!

Enliven, o my soul, your faith and if you are lacking in it, ask God and Mary of Good Success to grant it to you. Thus, by taking advantage of the special gift and singular privilege of having Mary of Good Success as our intercessor, we may not be responsible for a disdain or lack of appreciation for the gift that Providence has given us to increase our piety and encourage us in the practice of the virtues of faith, confidence, charity, obedience and the fulfillment of all our duties and obligations.

Prayer

O God, loving guardian of pious persons, families and Communities, Who in Thy Providence dost guard and protect them because of their attention to prayer and fulfillment of their duties of life, hear now our prayers. Be attentive to our cries, enflame the light of our faith in Thy powerful protection so that we do not fear our enemies. For if Thou assist us, nothing can harm us. Grant us an unlimited confidence in Mary Most Holy of Good Success and the grace of obedience to and observance of our Rule [or to the fulfillment of the duties of our particular state of life], so that we might be worthy of a Mother so holy and a Protectress so powerful. May we always be Thy grateful and docile subjects, so that one day we may sing with glory Thy praises in Heaven, Thou Who hast favored Mary as Daughter, Mother and Spouse of the Most Holy Trinity, the one God Who lives forever and ever. Amen.

Act of Thanksgiving to the Blessed Virgin
To be said each day of the novena

O Virgin blessed among all women! We lack the words to give thee thanks for the innumerable blessings that we have received from thy hand. The day of thy birth can be called the day of thanksgiving, happiness, and consolation. Thou art the honor of mankind, the joy of Paradise, the beloved gift of God, and the well-being of our country. What merit do we have, Blessed Virgin of Good Success, to deserve to have thee as our Mother? May God be forever blessed Who hath desired it so! Blessed also art thou, Virgin Mary, because despite our ingratitude, thou showest us thy propitious favor.

Thus art thou, most clement Mother, our consolation on earth, our refuge, our help, and our protection in both our public and private needs. Safeguard us from war, pestilence, hunger, storms, earthquakes, and all the calamities that we merit by our guilt. Pray for the Holy Church and for her visible head. Hear the supplications of those who invoke thee. Be thou our Advocate, our Mother, for as thus do we place our confidence in thee. To thee do we have recourse, and through thy intercession we hope to achieve from thy Son pardon for our sins and perseverance in grace until death. Amen.

Here, each one raising up his heart to God, should ask, through the intercession of Blessed Mary of Good Success, that grace or favor which he desires to receive.

Praises to the Holy Virgin
To be said each day of the novena

O Virgin Mary, our Mother preeminent above all on earth.
Response: *Come to our assistance and show us mercy, because thou art our Mother.*

Above all others, thou wert attentive to the Word of the Father, Who doth great things in thy honor.
Come to our assistance and show us mercy, because thou art our Mother.

Thou art the most worthy temple of the Most Holy Trinity.
Come to our assistance and show us mercy, because thou art our Mother.

In thee is that same purity the Angels enjoy.
Come to our assistance and show us mercy, because thou art our Mother.

The Christian world proclaims that thou dost reign on the right side of the King of Kings.
Come to our assistance and show us mercy, because thou art our Mother.

O Mother of Grace! O our hope! Port of the shipwrecked and star of the sea,
Come to our assistance and show us mercy, because thou art our Mother.

Gate of Heaven, health of the sick, light in the darkness.
Come to our assistance and show us mercy, because thou art our Mother.

Through thee, we will find ourselves before God in the court of the Saints, where He lives and reigns forever.
Come to our assistance and show us mercy, because thou art our Mother.

Guide our steps and help us, O sweet Mary, in our last hours.
Come to our assistance and show us mercy, because thou art our Mother.

Receive this praise from our tender lips, which cannot express thy singular grandeur.
Come to our assistance and show us mercy, because thou art our Mother.

Antiphon: Holy Mary, save the miserable, help the weak, intercede for the afflicted, plead for the people, intercede for the clergy, petition for the faithful. Permit all those who celebrate thy holy memory to experience thy favor and assistance.

> V. Pray for us, O Virgin of Good Success!
> R. That we may be made worthy of the promises of Christ.

Final Prayer

We ask thee, our Lord and God, that Thou grant us health of soul and body through the intercession of the glorious Virgin Mary. Through her merits and those of her sovereign Child Jesus, we hope to be freed from the present evils and to attain eternal happiness. Amen.

Day Nine
Novena to Our Lady of Good Success

Act of Repentence
To be said first, each day of the novena

I believe in Thee, O my God. Strengthen, O Lord, my faith. I hope in Thee, O my God. Affirm, O Lord, my hope. I love Thee, O my God; increase, O Lord, my love. I repent of having offended Thee. O my God, help me to have contrition, so that with the help of Thy grace and the powerful patronage of Holy Mary of Good Success, I may never sin again. O Lord, have pity and mercy on me. Amen.

Opening Prayer
To be said each day of the novena

O most Excellent and Immaculate Queen of Heaven, Holy Mary of Good Success, most favored Daughter of the Eternal Father, most beloved Mother of the Divine Son, most cherished Spouse of the Holy Spirit, sublime Throne of the Divine Majesty, August Temple of the Holy Trinity, in whom the Three Divine Persons have placed the treasures of Their Power, Wisdom and Love!

Remember, Virgin Mary of Good Success, whom God hath made so great so that thou canst give succor to miserable sinners; remember that thou hast often promised to show thyself a merciful Mother to those who have recourse to thee. I come to thee then, Mother most merciful, and I beg thee, for thy love of the Most High,

that thou should obtain for me from God the Father a lively Faith that never loses sight of the eternal truths; from the Son, a firm Hope that always aspires to reach that glory that He won for me with His Blood; and from the Holy Ghost, a charity so inflamed that I will always live loving the Supreme Goodness and thee, Most Holy Virgin, until through thy intervention I will love and enjoy thee eternally in glory. Amen.

We salute thee Mary, as the Favored Daughter of God the Father.
Hail Mary...

We salute thee Mary, as the Chosen Mother of the Divine Son.
Hail Mary...

We salute thee Mary, as the Singular Spouse of the Holy Ghost.
Hail Mary... Glory be to the Father...

Day Nine

Consider how the humble sister felt on hearing the command of Holy Mary, to have a statue made of the same size and appearance as the apparition. She excused herself saying that it would be impossible, that no sculptor could reproduce such rare beauty or render with precision its proper proportions. The beautiful Lady, with a most amiable forbearance, replied to her, "Do not fear for this reason. Take off the cord around your waist and measure my height."

Since, from a natural fear, the religious did not dare to touch Mary with her hands, the Heavenly Queen herself took the end of the cord and held it to her head, while the sister touched it to her feet to measure the exact height of the marvelous vision. Then Holy Mary said: "Here, as I told you, you have the height for the statue that you should order to be made, and the rest of the measurements should be in proportion to it. Place the statue in the place I have indicated with a crosier and the keys of the cloister in my right hand, for I desire to be Advocate and Protectress of this Convent." Having said this, the vision disappeared.

The heart of the sister who had just received such a signal favor and so pleasing a mission was penetrated, filled with gratitude and warm sentiments for Mary Most Holy! O my soul, search in your heart for those sentiments, and be dissolved in gratitude for Mary of Good Success, our Advocate and Protectress. Let me venerate her Image with the most tender gratitude and the vehement desire of corresponding to such singular benefits by leading a life that is holy, obedient, and observant of all the duties of my state of life.

Then the holy sister who had been favored with this vision made efforts to find an accomplished sculptor to begin the work on this statue that Mary herself had ordered to be made. Thus this statue, full of sweetness and majesty, will last until the end of time. Venerated in the upper choir of this Convent, the religious there always have recourse to her in their most grave conflicts. So also has she been the refuge of all people who come to her in their necessities, and through her intercession many portentous favors and special graces have been obtained.

The measurements given by Mary symbolize the measure of her humility, obedience, and love of God and neighbor, which she gives to us so that we might strive to reproduce them. Imitate her, and you will carry an image of the Virgin Most Holy in your heart. Strive like that holy sister to make the moral image of your Virgin Mother in your customs and sentiments, in your bearing and way of acting, in your fidelity to your daily duties and prayers, in your meekness and candor, in your purity and detachment from earthly things, thus aspiring only to heavenly goods.

Prayer

Oh God! Tender Father of Thy creatures Who in every manner demonstrates Thy paternal care and guidance for us, principally by giving us Mary Most Holy as our advocate, protectress, and model ideal of virtue, infuse our hearts with a constant desire to imitate our Mother and Queen, modeling our thoughts, desires, and actions after those of Mary Most Holy so that we might be like Her in all that our fragile nature permits. Assisted by Thy Divine Grace, may we conquer our passions and receive the choicest graces that our Mother grants to her children who confidently come to her as Advocate in their pressing needs. May we find her ready to assist us in the last difficult moment of life, and afterward enjoy the pleasure of her company in Heaven forever and ever. Amen

Act of Thanksgiving to the Blessed Virgin
To be said each day of the novena

O Virgin blessed among all women! We lack the words to give thee thanks for the innumerable blessings that we have received from thy hand. The day of thy birth can be called the day of thanksgiving, happiness, and consolation. Thou art the honor of mankind, the joy of Paradise, the beloved gift of God, and the well-being of our country. What merit do we have, Blessed Virgin of Good Success, to deserve to have thee as our Mother? May God be forever blessed Who hath desired it so! Blessed also art thou, Virgin Mary, because despite our ingratitude, thou showest us thy propitious favor.

Thus art thou, most clement Mother, our consolation on earth, our refuge, our help, and our protection in both our public and private needs. Safeguard us from war, pestilence, hunger, storms, earthquakes, and all the calamities that we merit by our guilt. Pray for the Holy Church and for her visible head. Hear the supplications of those who invoke thee. Be thou our Advocate, our Mother, for as thus do we place our confidence in thee. To thee do we have recourse, and through thy intercession we hope to achieve from thy Son pardon for our sins and perseverance in grace until death. Amen.

Here, each one raising up his heart to God, should ask, through the intercession of Blessed Mary of Good Success, that grace or favor which he desires to receive.

Praises to the Holy Virgin
To be said each day of the novena

O Virgin Mary, our Mother preeminent above all on earth.
Response: *Come to our assistance and show us mercy, because thou art our Mother.*

Above all others, thou wert attentive to the Word of the Father, Who doth great things in thy honor.
Come to our assistance and show us mercy, because thou art our Mother.

Thou art the most worthy temple of the Most Holy Trinity.
Come to our assistance and show us mercy, because thou art our Mother.

In thee is that same purity the Angels enjoy.
Come to our assistance and show us mercy, because thou art our Mother.

The Christian world proclaims that thou dost reign on the right side of the King of Kings.
Come to our assistance and show us mercy, because thou art our Mother.

O Mother of Grace! O our hope! Port of the shipwrecked and star of the sea,
Come to our assistance and show us mercy, because thou art our Mother.

Gate of Heaven, health of the sick, light in the darkness.
Come to our assistance and show us mercy, because thou art our Mother.

Through thee, we will find ourselves before God in the court of the Saints, where He lives and reigns forever.
Come to our assistance and show us mercy, because thou art our Mother.

Guide our steps and help us, O sweet Mary, in our last hours.
Come to our assistance and show us mercy, because thou art our Mother.

Receive this praise from our tender lips, which cannot express thy singular grandeur.
Come to our assistance and show us mercy, because thou art our Mother.

Antiphon: Holy Mary, save the miserable, help the weak, intercede for the afflicted, plead for the people, intercede for the clergy, petition for the faithful. Permit all those who celebrate thy holy memory to experience thy favor and assistance.

   V. Pray for us, O Virgin of Good Success!
   R. *That we may be made worthy of the promises of Christ.*

Final Prayer

We ask thee, our Lord and God, that Thou grant us health of soul and body through the intercession of the glorious Virgin Mary. Through her merits and those of her sovereign Child Jesus, we hope to be freed from the present evils and to attain eternal happiness. Amen.

The novena by Fr. José M. Urrate, S.J. has an *Imprimatur* by the Archbishop of Quito Carlos Maria, issued from the Ecclesiastical Government of the Archdiocese of Quito on July 31, 1941.

Made in the USA
Monee, IL
31 January 2022